NEW ZEALAND

FIRST TO SEE THE DAWN

NEW ZEALAND

FIRST TO SEE THE DAWN

REED

Published by Reed Books, a division of Reed Publishing (NZ) Ltd, 39 Rawene Rd, Birkenhead, Auckland. Associated companies, branches and representatives throughout the world.

Established in 1907, Reed Publishing (NZ) Ltd
is New Zealand's largest book publisher, with over 300 titles in print.

For details on all these books visit our website:
www.reed.co.nz

ISBN 0 7900 0711 8
First published 1997
Reprinted 1998, 2000

Front cover photograph: Dawn by Charles Cooper.
Title page: Marokopa Falls, Waikato

All photographs by Holger Leue except:
Bob McCree: pages 17, 18, 19, 22 (lower), 66, 83
Charles Cooper: page 24 (both)
Peter Janssen: pages 28 (both), 30 (upper), 56, 59 (both)
Ian Baker: pages 61 (upper), 67 (both), 88
Collection Museum of New Zealand Te Papa Tongarewa, F.4960/03: page 75
Carolyn Lagahetau: page 126 (upper), 130 (upper)

Printed by Everbest,China

Te Reinga to Auckland **6**

Waikato to the Volcanic Plateau **26**

46

Coromandel to the Wairarapa

Taranaki to Wellington **64**

Marlborough and Nelson to Kaikoura

76

Christchurch and Canterbury **88**

The West Coast **104**

Dunedin and Otago **120**

Murihiku: The South **138**

Acknowledgements **160**

Contents

The gateway to Auckland's Aotea
Centre, the work of Maori artist
Selwyn Muru.

Te Reinga to Auckland

Tradition has it that Northland is where Kupe, the Maori discoverer of Aotearoa, landed. When he took the news back to the legendary Hawaiki it was of a place of sunshine, beauty and incredible potential. The east coast is a complex of deep harbours with names that roll off the tongue like breakers coming in from the sea — Parengarenga, Houhora, Kerikeri — down to Whangarei, the main city of the north. The west coast is a maze of estuaries and shallow harbours, dominated by the Hokianga Harbour. Everywhere there are long sandy beaches and small sun-baked settlements snoozing in the sun.

Once upon a time the rugged hills were totally covered with the kauri, King of Trees; although the majority were felled for the early shipbuilding industry there are still some stands remaining to remind us of the imposing forests that touched the sky. Other places are haunted with memories of the kauri gumlands, where Maori and Dalmatian worked together.

The Bay of Islands was the cradle of both Maori and Pakeha settlement and it was here that the Treaty of Waitangi was signed in 1840. From the grounds of the Treaty House you can look across to Paihia and Russell. Nearby Okiato was the site of New Zealand's first capital, although this was soon moved to Auckland.

Sprawled across the isthmus between the Manukau and Waitemata Harbours, Auckland has grown from a shantytown on the beach to become New Zealand's largest city, and the largest Polynesian city in the world.

Today Auckland is in fact four cities — Auckland City itself, North Shore City, Manukau City and Waitakere City. The centrepiece of Auckland City is Queen Street, which runs up from the harbour to Karangahape Road, but throughout there are suburbs of distinctive charm and individuality. The dance clubs and restaurants of Ponsonby, Herne Bay, Parnell, Mission Bay and Devonport are always busy, while the Polynesian markets of South Auckland are vibrant and alive.

Auckland's natural configuration is complicated by volcanic cones, the most dramatic of which is Rangitoto Island. More than any other feature, Rangitoto is a physical icon for Aucklanders, symbolising their love of the outdoors and their wonderful harbour.

Native flax provides a graphic
foreground to the Hokianga Harbour,
on Northland's west coast.

Kerikeri was the second Anglican
mission station in Aotearoa New
Zealand, and the Stone Store is the
oldest surviving stone building in the
country. Nearby are the beautiful
Rainbow Falls. Orchards abound near
Kerikeri, the country's premier citrus-
growing area.

Once a haven for tall whaling ships, the Bay of Islands is still a favourite destination of sailors, sunseekers and fishers. Cruises include the Fullers Mailboat, which delivers mail to the more isolated bays of the coast, and the fascinating Hole in the Rock. Later on, where better to relax than Russell's historic Duke of Marlborough Hotel?

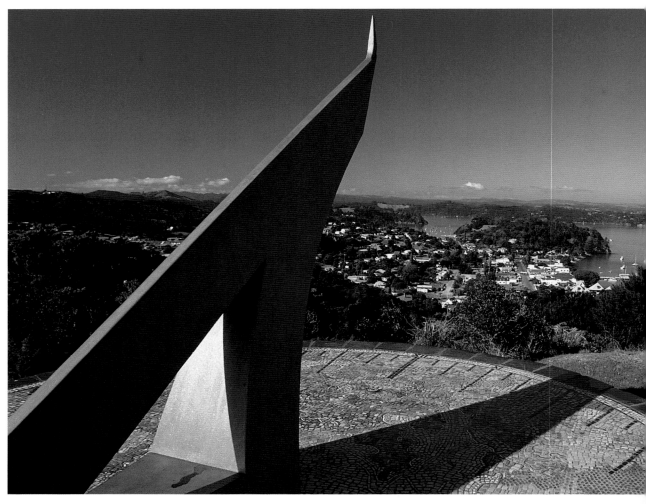

The sundial on Russell's Flagstaff Hill overlooks the town and the superb Bay of Islands.

Pompallier House, which stands on Russell's waterfront, is now a museum illustrating the early days of Russell and the French mission which was based here under Bishop Pompallier. Traditional printing crafts are now undertaken here, recreating the mission's major activity last century.

In 1840 the Treaty of Waitangi was
signed by the British and a number of
local Maori chiefs. The Treaty House
itself dates from 1833 and served as the
home to the first British resident, James
Busby, who helped negotiate the Treaty.
The whare runanga (meeting house) is
unusual in that it incorporates carvings
from tribes throughout New Zealand.
Also in the grounds stands Tokimata-
whaorua, a seagoing waka (canoe).

Auckland is New Zealand's largest city.
The Sky City Tower is a dominant part
of the skyline at 328 metres, taller than
both the Eiffel Tower and the Centre-
point Tower in Sydney. Sitting astride
the Waitemata and Manukau harbours,
Auckland is a boater's paradise.

Built in 1929, Auckland's Civic Theatre is an
architecturally elegant host to both movies
and moviegoers. Further along Queen Street
a pavement artist attracts a crowd who
admire his work.

The city is connected to the North Shore
suburbs by the Harbour Bridge, built in
1959, with extra lanes added by Japanese
engineers (and wittily referred to as 'the
Nippon clip-on').

From the volcanic cone of Mt Eden, the
island of Rangitoto provides a sculpted
backdrop to the city below. On Auckland
city's waterfront, the America's Cup Village
is surrounded by bars, restaurants and cafes
to suit all tastes. Further along the waterfront, at Kelly Tarlton's Underwater World
spectators can travel through transparent
tunnels within a giant aquarium and visit
penguins in the Antarctic exhibit.

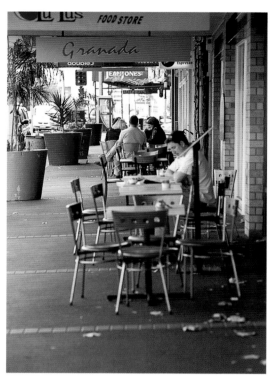

The cafes, restaurants and bars along Ponsonby Road reflect New Zealand's diverse styles of cuisine. Below, at the Auckland War Memorial Museum visitors can explore all facets of New Zealand's history, as well as seeing contemporary travelling exhibitions of local and overseas arts and crafts.

25

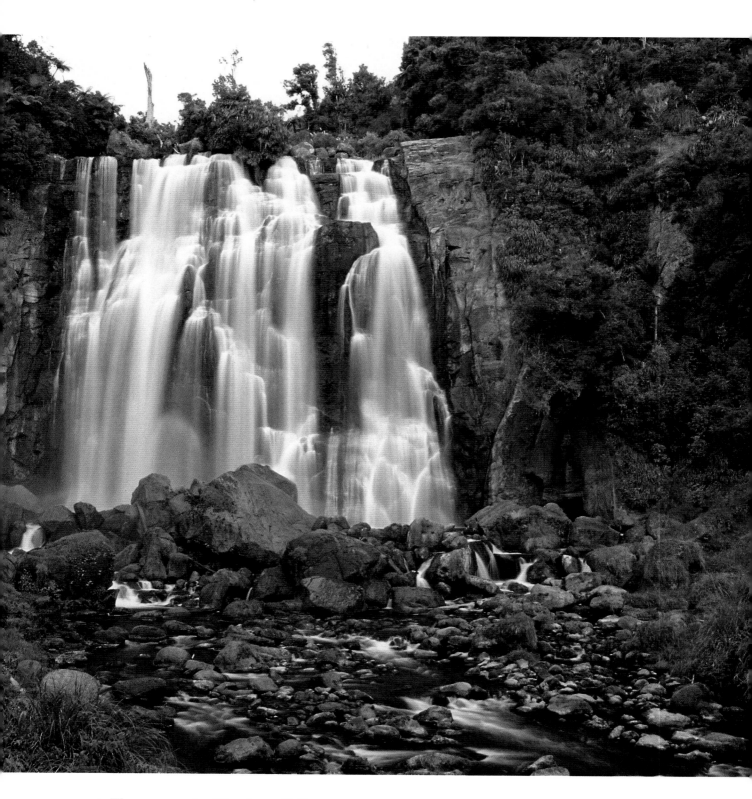

The spectacular Marokopa Falls, near
Te Anga, in the Waikato.

Waikato to the Volcanic Plateau

During the Land Wars of the 1860s the Maori King Tawhiao threw his hat on a map of New Zealand and said, 'Where the hat lands I will protect all those who have given offence to the Queen of England.' The hat landed on the King Country, an area of limestone, which accounts for its often amazing topography of crags, ravines, canyons and caves. One such formation has become one of the great subterranean wonders of the world — the Waitomo Caves. The spectacular Glow-Worm Grotto shimmers with a million tiny lights like a miniature heaven.

The stronghold of the Maori Kings is in the Waikato on the Turangawaewae marae at Ngaruawahia. Not far away is Taupiri Mountain, where the Maori Kings are buried. Through this landscape winds the mighty Waikato River. Each year in March war canoes sail on the river as part of an annual celebration of Kingitanga, the heritage of the Maori King movement.

Right at the heart of the North Island is the Volcanic Plateau. The volcanic area actually runs from White Island on the east coast diagonally through Rotorua down to Taupo and the mountains of Tongariro National Park.

At Whakarewarewa Village, in Rotorua, Maori culture forms part of a theatrical backdrop of mudpools, hot springs, drifting steam and spouting geysers. If you want to be reminded of a more ferocious aspect of the area visit Waiotapu or the Waimangu Valley. In this region, in 1886, Mount Tarawera erupted, destroying the fabulous Pink and White Terraces. Drive on to Taupo, and when you swim in the lake, go yachting or fish for trout, just remember that once upon a time this was a volcano that blew its top.

Hamilton is surrounded
by some of the country's
richest farmland. The
city is intersected by the
country's longest river,
the Waikato. Home to the
University of Waikato,
the area is also
renowned for the quality
of its agricultural
research and
development.

At Waitomo, in the King Country, sightseers come from all over the world to visit the magnificent Waitomo Caves, one of the world's natural wonders. The traditional boat journey will take you through the caves, or you can join a blackwater rafting tour to explore this underground world in more adventurous fashion.

The Karapiro dam system provides much of the North Island's electricity. Lake Karapiro is also world-renowned as a rowing venue and has excellent areas for water-skiing and trout fishing.

The city of Rotorua, with its ever-present smell of hydrogen sulphide, is at the heart of a region known for its spectacular volcanic beauty. Among its

many attractions is the historic
bathhouse in the Government Gardens,
home of the Rotorua Art and History
Museum. Also of interest is the
Agrodome, which regularly features
demonstrations of sheep shearing and
dog working.

Rotorua's Whakarewarewa Reserve is a major centre of Maori culture and has become an important school of learning for Maori craftsmen and women. At its entrance visitors practise the hongi, the traditional Maori greeting. The carvings on the meeting house have a special significance for the local people.

The Te Arawa people are well known for their spectacular singing and dancing. Women practise the art of poi dancing and men perform the haka. Traditional stories are told in the movements and actions that accompany the songs.

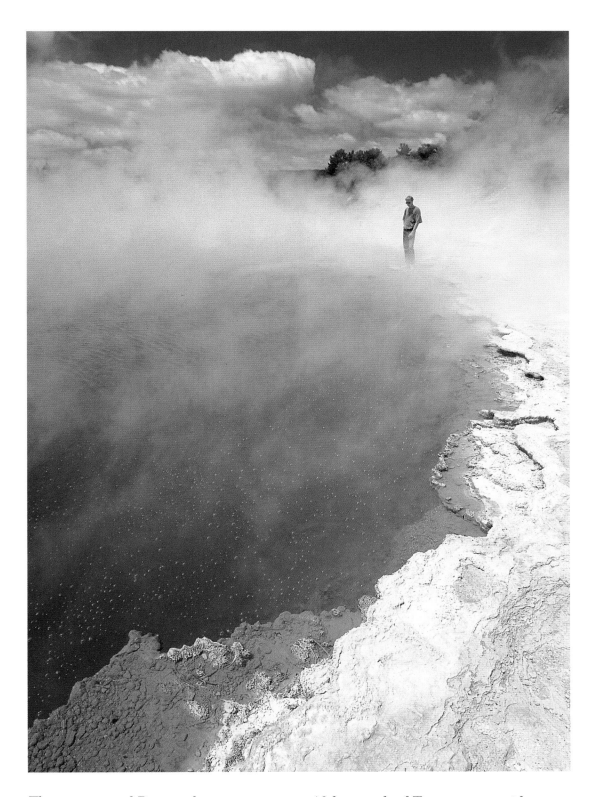

The area around Rotorua boasts an amazing variety of thermal activity. While the geysers and mudpools at Whakarewarewa (opposite, bottom) are well known, a visit to the Wairakei Thermal Valley (opposite, top) just 10 km north of Taupo can provide an equally dramatic experience of steam and bubbling mud. Halfway between Rotorua and Taupo the colourful Champagne Pool (above) is one of the attractions of Waiotapu Scenic Reserve.

Across Lake Tarawera can be seen the
famous Mt Tarawera, which on 10 June
1886 exploded, destroying the fabulous
Pink and White Terraces

Steam rises from the Wairakei
geothermal power station, the second
largest in the world. The awesome
power of the earth's natural resources
can also be seen at the mighty Huka
Falls, on the Waikato River, a little
nearer Taupo.

New Zealanders and visitors from all
over the world come to fish the waters
of Lake Taupo and ski the slopes of Mt
Ruapehu, whose warm crater lake looks
deceptively quiet in the afternoon sun.
Although the mountain has not erupted
in recent times, it is still an active
volcano. At the foot of the mountain
stands The Grand Chateau, with Mt
Ngauruhoe beyond.

43

Mt Ngauruhoe at sunrise, obscured by
the swirling clouds.

Late afternoon near Port Jackson,
Coromandel Peninsula.

Coromandel to the Wairarapa

Before the coming of the Pakeha, Coromandel provided an impenetrable screen of lush fern and kauri forest. Like the Northland forests, however, the kauri of Coromandel were soon felled for the ship-building industry. Gold was discovered at Thames and Waihi in 1867, and the gold industry flourished until early this century. Today gold is once again being mined at Waihi, but Coromandel is better known for the golden sand of its beaches and the wild beauty of its peninsula.

The shoreline of the Bay of Plenty can take your breath away, especially when pohutukawa blossoms in the summer. When Europeans settled the area it was developed into sheep and cattle country, but today oranges, kiwifruit and grapes have taken over. The harvest is shipped to markets around the world.

South of the Bay of Plenty is East Cape. For a time whaling flourished along the coast, but today's pursuits are primarily fishing, sheep and cattle grazing, and forestry. The settlements haven't changed much since the old days, resembling frontier towns out of a Western movie.

The beaches around the Cape, Poverty Bay and down through Hawke's Bay are among the most magnificent in New Zealand, and the whole coast resonates with history, both Maori and Pakeha. Some of the biggest Maori meeting houses are found here, and some of the North Island's most graceful colonial houses.

Inland from the Cape are the mysterious Ureweras, home of the Tuhoe people, the Children of the Mist. Their kingdom is a mountain fortress guarded by rocky terrain, silver waterfalls and lakes.

Hawke's Bay is the home of some of New Zealand's great sheep stations. More recently its climate has encouraged diversification into horticulture, market gardening and orcharding. Half of New Zealand's wine is made in Hawke's Bay. The twin cities of the area, Napier and Hastings, were severely damaged in an earthquake in 1931. Napier was reconstructed in the angular, jazzy, Art Deco style and today is known as the Art Deco Capital of the World.

Then there's the Wairarapa, the centre of New Zealand's Scandinavian community, and a strong agricultural region. The main city of the Wairarapa is Masterton, while nearby Martinborough is the centre of a growing wine industry.

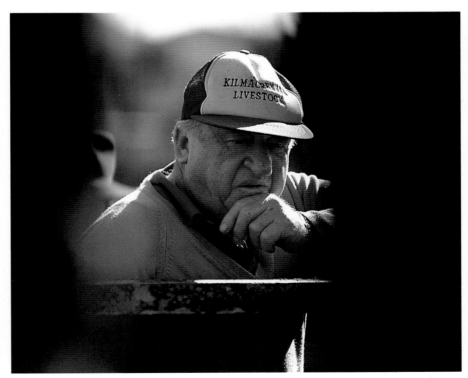

The deserted peace of Cathedral Cove, near Hahei, on the Coromandel Peninsula, contrasts with the gentle clamour of a livestock auction at nearby Coroglen.

Driving Creek railway, the creation of
potter Barry Brickell, winds up through
the brilliant green of the bush to a view
across the Coromandel valley.

The east coast of the Coromandel
Peninsula looks straight across the ocean
to the place where the sun rises. Here at
Opoutere the sunrises are dramatic, with
colours ranging from delicate ochres and
pinks to cerise, violet and vermillion.

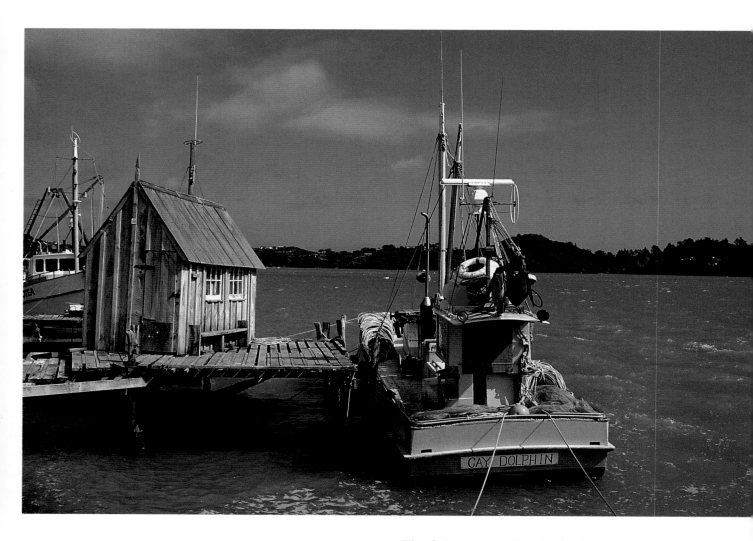

The fishing boat *Gay Dolphin* tosses in Coromandel Harbour in a sea quickening with the tide. At Thames memories abound of the gold rushes of the 1860s and '70s, when the town's population reached 20,000, almost twice that of Auckland. The Brian Boru Hotel, one of the few remaining accommodation houses, is best known today for its Murder Mystery weekends.

White Island, in the Bay of Plenty, occasionally sends up steam and lava just to remind us that it is still an active volcano.

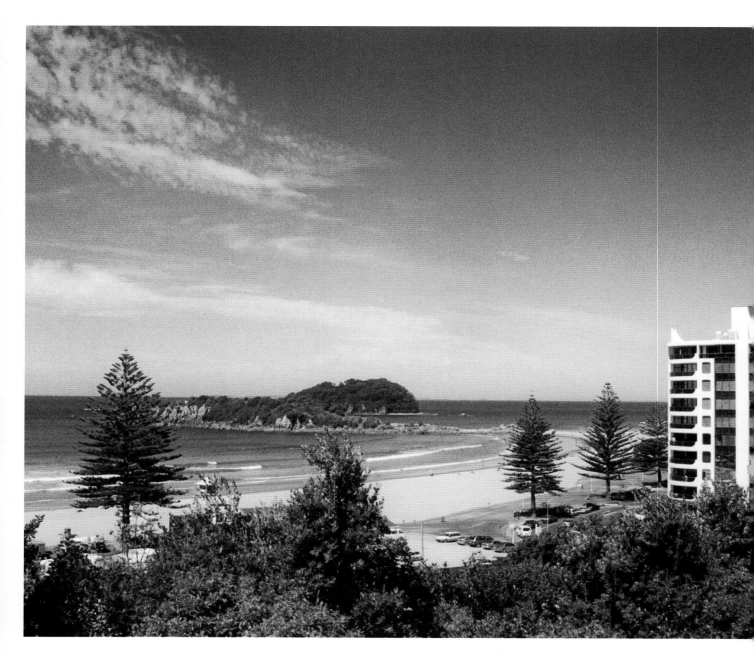

Mt Maunganui, famous for its surf, is a favourite summer holiday spot in the sunny Bay of Plenty.

On the wall of a fish and chip shop at Katikati, a family poses outside a typical Bay of Plenty church, as if waiting for a photograph to be taken. On the beach near Opotiki, two Maori seek the succulent pipi, a shellfish regarded as a delicacy.

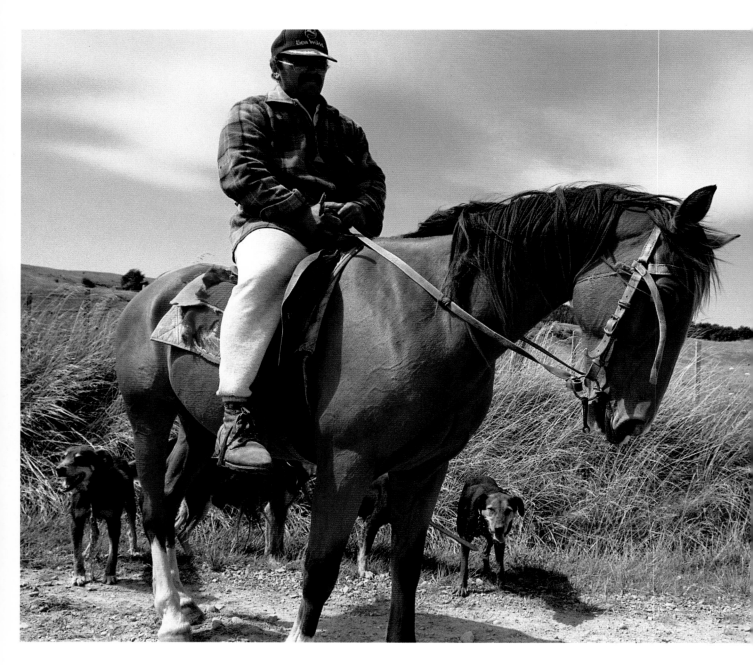

The East Coast has a relaxed lifestyle,
and the drive around the coast is for
those with plenty of time, who are
happy to leave themselves open to
whatever happens next. At the north
end of Poverty Bay, at the junction of
two rivers and within easy reach of
beautiful beaches, lies Gisborne. Within
the city are many beautiful parks and
the city's main street, Gladstone Road, is
adorned by an impressive clock tower.

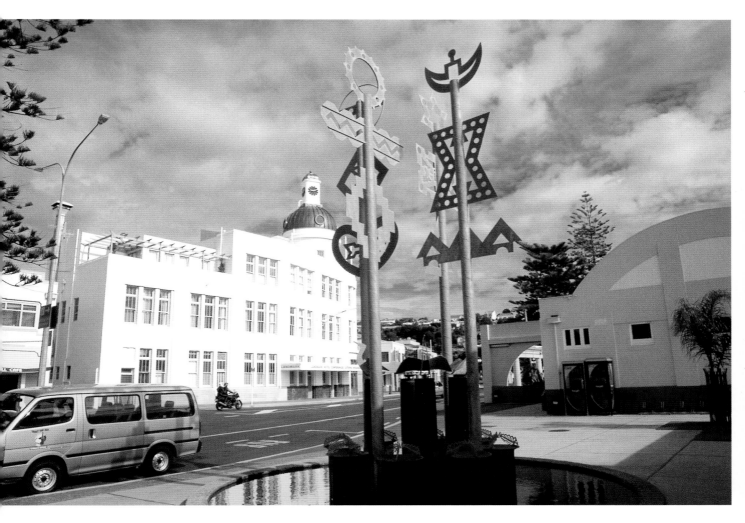

A dolphin leaps during a sea world display at Marineland, Napier. The city is famous for its Art Deco buildings, attracting many visitors throughout the year. The annual Art Deco weekend attracts interest from around the world and celebrates the city's unique style.

Castlepoint Lighthouse, east of
Masterton, signals a warning to ships off
the wild Wairarapa coast. A fishing boat
shelters in the lee of the headland.

Mt Taranaki (also known as Mt
Egmont) has a reputation for being New
Zealand's most climbed mountain. The
mountain's dominance is more than
visual, as the Taranaki province, in part,
owes its fertile land to its volcanic ash.

Taranaki to Wellington

On a clear day, Taranaki (also known as Mt Egmont) can be seen from the South Island. It made itself known to the earliest Maori canoe voyagers but when Abel Tasman sailed past in 1642 it hid itself from him. However, for James Cook in 1770 Taranaki was kinder. He saw it through cloud and rain, with lightning dancing around its crown. In 1841 ships of the New Zealand Company arrived from England's Plymouth and, within the gaze of Taranaki, established the settlement of New Plymouth.

From the summit of Taranaki you feel as if you can see the world. Ruapehu, Taranaki's brother mountain, is eastward. Seaward is a curve of black sand, like a fin flicking at the deep blue of the Tasman Sea. Below, the rainforest carpets the flanks of the mountain, and beyond the plains roll towards New Plymouth and Hawera to the south. Offshore, oil rigs dot the Taranaki Bight.

To the south, the deep gorges, waterfalls and wilderness of the Whanganui River have a special attraction for those who would explore it by canoe, white-river raft or jetboat. The Rangitikei and Manawatu rivers, further inland, are just as stunning. At the seaward end of the Manawatu gorge is the largest city of the plains, Palmerston North. For many years a university town, today Palmerston North is also a centre for agricultural and horticultural research, and for wider education.

Wellington, the capital, is one of New Zealand's most cultured and vibrant cities. The suburbs of Wellington all retain their own special character. Newtown, for example, is a mix of Maori, Pacific Island, Greek and new immigrant families, creating a joyful blend of fun and excitement. In recent years the waterfront and inner city have been transformed into a showcase of art, music, theatre and culture. Innovative architecture has added a new and exciting look to the city, contrasting with the older, gentler areas of Mount Victoria and Tinakori Road.

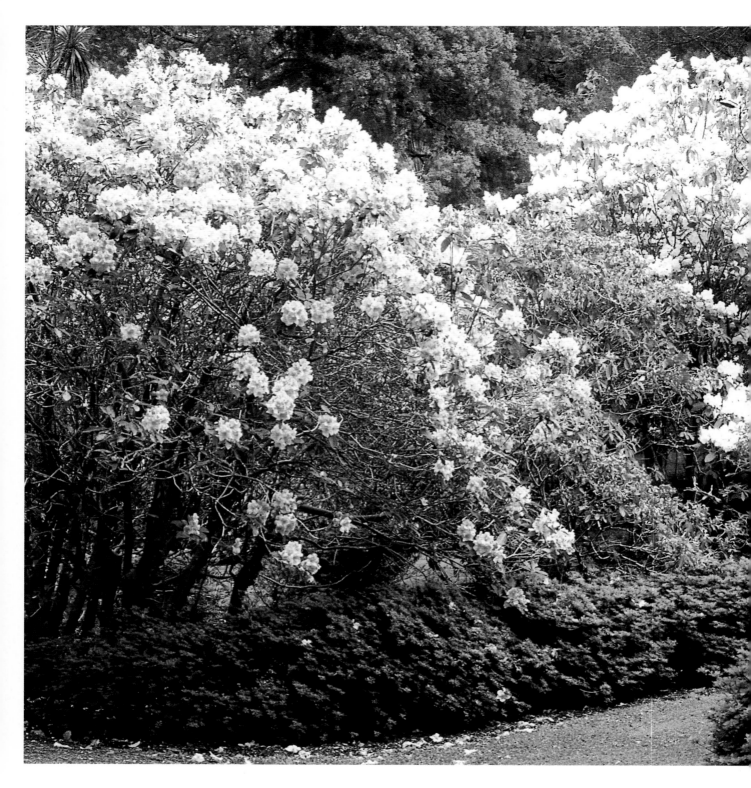

New Plymouth city has become the focus of oil based
industries in New Zealand as well as maintaining its
important role in agricultural development. Pukekura
Park, a must see when visiting the city, was once
wasteland and was converted to its present beauty by
volunteer labour.

Wanganui, one of New Zealand's oldest cities, charms visitors with its mature gardens and fascinating heritage, some of which can be viewed at the Wanganui Regional Museum. The city is established around the Whanganui River, which formerly provided a coastal port link with Wellington and New Plymouth. Further south, Palmerston North is home to many hectares of splendid parks, and is also home to a number of agricultural research centres, including Massey University.

Whanganui National Park, which opened in 1987, encompasses 79,000 hectares of lowland forest on both sides of the Whanganui River. The Park is popular with trampers, many of whom head for the Bridge to Nowhere. Built in 1936, the bridge was never fully utilised as many settlers were abandoning the area by the time of its completion. Today the area's main industry is tourism, and the river provides exciting jet-boating and canoeing adventures.

Low sun illuminates Oriental Bay, one of Wellington's most attracti... suburbs

Wellington's Beehive is an addition
to the old Parliament Buildings.
Opened in 1981, it was inspired, so
people say, by the logo on a box of
matches.

The Cable Car provides a swift,
steep ride from the inner city, seen
here from Tinakori Hill, to the
university suburb of Kelburn.

The Wellington skyline has been transformed in recent years, with a number of striking new buildings. Wellingtonians are particularly proud of their Civic Square, with its paved courtyard and tiled fountains. The Museum of New Zealand, Te Papa Tongarewa is a stunning building both inside and out. As well as housing exhibits that explore and explain many aspects of New Zealand's history and culture, the museum also plays host to travelling exhibitions from other parts of the country and the world.

The Marlborough Sounds offer glorious isolation, a calm haven in which to escape from the pressures of the world.

Marlborough and Nelson to Kaikoura

The Marlborough Sounds are magical sea-filled valleys which provide spectacular sailing and swimming. Their shores are clothed with unspoilt bush. Some of the islands further out are home to New Zealand's tuatara, a living link back to the dinosaurs of old.

Inland from the Sounds, the perspective changes. High tussock and alpine country overlook gentle river valleys and the sprawling Wairau Plains. Marlborough was once the home of great sheep stations, but today orchards, vineyards and berry fields dominate the landscape. The soil, and the sun, are particularly conducive to fine wine production and as a result Marlborough is home to some of New Zealand's best, and biggest, wineries.

West of Marlborough is Nelson, described by Abel Tasman in 1642 as 'a great land uplifted high'. Nelson shares with Blenheim one of the best climates in the country. Its beaches are golden sand swept by sparkling sea, the townships are colourful and friendly, and fruit trees, vines and berries flourish amid valleys of trees and ferns.

Nelson City, established by the New Zealand Company in 1842, is the centre of the province. Today it is a delightful mix of modernity and old world charm. Although its traditional industry remains horticulture, the area's rich fishing grounds have now turned Nelson into the biggest fishing port in New Zealand. The city is also a magnet for artisans — jewellers, potters, glassworkers and sculptors — who create some of New Zealand's finest craftworks. Close by is Abel Tasman National Park, a wonderful area of golden beaches, steep granite formations, limestone caves and native forest.

The Kaikoura coast follows the Pacific seaboard all the way down to Canterbury. Whaling was once a major industry along the coast. Today, the more gentle art of whalewatching provides an opportunity to witness some of the world's most beautiful creatures.

The hills surrounding the Marlborough Sounds are dotted with holiday homes, many of them reached by boat. During the still evenings the area is alive with the sounds of sea and forest. Among the most distinctive songsters of the region is the weka, a small flightless bird about the size of a domestic hen.

Lake Rotoroa, the larger of the two
lakes of Nelson Lakes National Park.

The sun, surf and wind make Abel
Tasman National Park ideal for yachting, windsurfing and sea kayaking, or
simply lazing on its lovely beaches.
Above, Nelson city is recognised as the
geographical centre of New Zealand and
also claims to be the 'sunshine capital'
of the country.

Many who visit Kaikoura come by train, enjoying the scenic coastal route. The area is famous for its kai moana, or seafood.

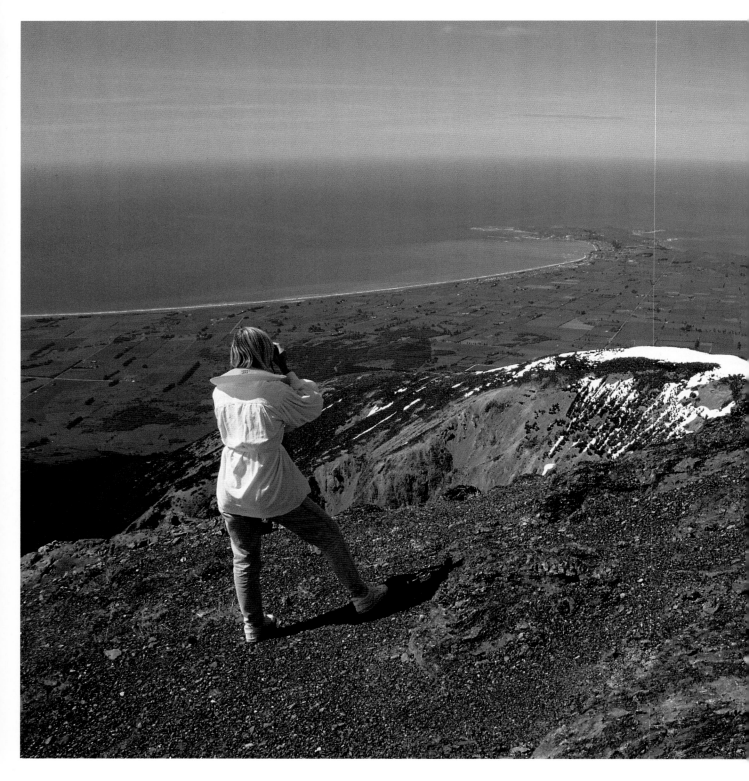

The view from Mount Fyffe, named
after a pioneer whaler. Today it is whale
watching that draws visitors to
Kaikoura, as well as adventure activities
such as paragliding.

Akaroa was founded in 1840 and was the only French colony in the country. The town has traces of its origins in its early architecture. However, the village is predominantly late Victorian in style and well worth the time and effort to visit.

Christchurch and Canterbury

T he landscape of Canterbury is dominated by its mountains. They are sentinels of the southern sky, with passes like narrow gateways through to the West Coast. For the traveller they provide an everchanging vista of immense power and beauty. New Zealand's longest glacier, the Tasman, is located in Mt Cook National Park. Ski-planes regularly set down skiers at the top of the glacier for a fabulous run down a magical river of ice and snow.

The immense Canterbury Plains, once the home of the giant moa, seem to roll on forever. From the air, the plains look like a vast pastoral ocean of patchwork green and gold, interrupted every now and then by the blue-grey of an intricately braided river.

In 1840 the French established a settlement at Akaroa, on Banks Peninsula, a township which today still maintains a piquant Gallic flavour. But it wasn't until 1848 and the establishment of the Canterbury Association in London that the idea of founding an Anglican settlement in New Zealand was formulated. Two years later, in 1850, four ships — the *Randolph, Charlotte Jane, Cressy* and *Sir George Seymour* — landed at Lyttelton. The idea was to transpose a model English society, complete with bishop, gentry, tradespeople and other workers, people known for their respectability and high morals. The result was a South Seas version of Britain that has no parallel in New Zealand.

Nowhere is this more apparent than in Christchurch, the largest city of the South Island. The cathedral triumphs in the centre, and church spires spike the sky. Amid drifting willows the river Avon wends its way through a city of Gothic architecture and ever-changing colours. The green banks and parks blossom with flowers in spring, transforming the city into a colourful garden. Walk around the old university buildings, now transformed into an Arts Centre, or visit some of the city's older schools, splendid amid leafy settings, and you would think you were in an English university town.

There is, of course, also a 'new' Christchurch, vibrant and ambitious, which reminds you quite firmly that the city is looking very much to the future. A busy airport, a growing reputation as an industrial city utilising the best of modern technology, and progressive city planning have made Christchurch one of the most positive of New Zealand's cities.

Cambridge? No, punting on the River Avon, Kiwi-style. The river winds its way through the city of Christchurch, past the modern Town Hall with its ingenious fountain, and the nearby Floral Clock.

Christchurch's Cathedral Square is
always alive with activity. Buskers
entertain, people sit and watch the
crowds pass by, and the city's Wizard
declaims.

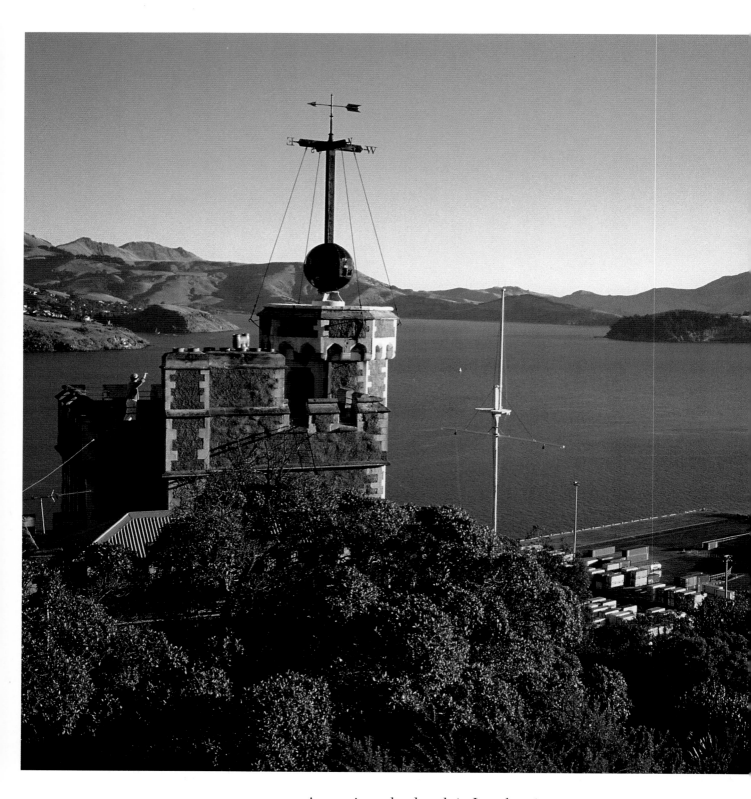

A prominent landmark in Lyttelton is
the Timeball Station, its Victorian
mechanism signalling the time to ships
in the harbour by the dropping of a ball
down the mast on the top of the tower.

Christ's College, founded on the principles of an English public school, is one of the country's oldest.

Two cyclists on Summit Road, the rim of the Port Hills, watch the sun set over Christchurch.

A large mural, painted on the side of
the Fire Station at Lake Tekapo,
acknowledges the place of sheep in the
colourful history of the Mackenzie
country.

The Church of the Good Shepherd, at Lake Tekapo, was built in acknowledgement of the sacrifices of the early runholders of the area. The sheepdogs of the Mackenzie country are also honoured here.

Sheep graze on winter pasture beside
Lake Tekapo, South Canterbury.

Within Mount Cook National Park, scenic flights over
the Southern Alps are popular, with one landing site on
the Tasman Glacier. The glacier is 27 kilometres long
and is kin to the mighty Mt Cook, 3753 metres high
and New Zealand's highest mountain.

From the snow-capped peaks and
glaciers, water drains into the braided
rivers on both sides of the Main Divide,
and forms lakes such as Pukaki, a vital
part of the Upper Waitaki Power
Development Scheme.

A glimpse of what lies ahead, the
coastline of the West Coast.

The West Coast

The West Coast is rather like a forest fortress, its mountain peaks palisades guarding against all-comers. A constant curtain of rain provides an extra layer of protection. Were it not for the fabled greenstone, or pounamu, perhaps the Maori would never have come here, to the great Westland rivers, the Arahura and the Taramakau.

Later, another kind of stone, gold, brought Europeans into the area. Ironically, the gold was found beneath a greenstone boulder by Maori who were more interested in the pounamu. This was in 1864. A year later gold mining began in Hokitika and Reefton. Even later, another mineral, coal, added to the region's prosperity.

The goldmining days brought a sense of the frontier to the West Coast. Perhaps it is because of this that Coasters are considered different from other New Zealanders. Not any better or worse, just a bit different — irreverent, enterprising, sometimes stubborn, but always decent. In many respects they are the archetypal 'good keen men' and independent women of New Zealand's ideal society, having a healthy disrespect for authority and relying more on their own sense of what's right and what isn't.

One of the most dominant features of the West Coast is the opalescent sea, which seems to carry on a constant love affair with the coast. The whole of the West Coast is a place of whispers, of sounds and mysteries, offering moments of sheer beauty as when a white heron feathers the air at its nesting place at Okarito.

It is also a place of immense silence. The beaches are unpopulated and the emerald green forests are isolated. Nowhere is the silence more profound than at the two rivers of ice — the Fox and Franz Josef Glaciers. Sometimes, in the gleaming half-light of day, they defy reality and render the surrounding landscape unreal also.

The astonishing Pancake Rocks, at
Punakaiki, lie within one of New
Zealand's newest national parks,
Paparoa. Nearby the rich red of the
pohutukawa flower adds a vivid splash
of colour to the bush. A little further
south, a cyclist sets out on the road to
adventure.

107

108

During the latter part of the nineteenth century Okarito was alive with pubs, dance halls, casinos, banks and stores, as miners flocked to join the search for gold on the Coast. Today it is a quieter place, sought for its detachment from the world, and the allure of its whitebait.

A canoeist shares the peace of Okarito Lagoon with a rare white heron, or kotuku. The only breeding ground of the kotuku is on the banks of the nearby Waitangiroto Stream.

Guided walking tours take visitors right
on to the magnificent Fox and Franz
Josef Glaciers. At close quarters these
shining rivers of ice ripple with blue and
green colours and reveal jumbled blocks
of ice.

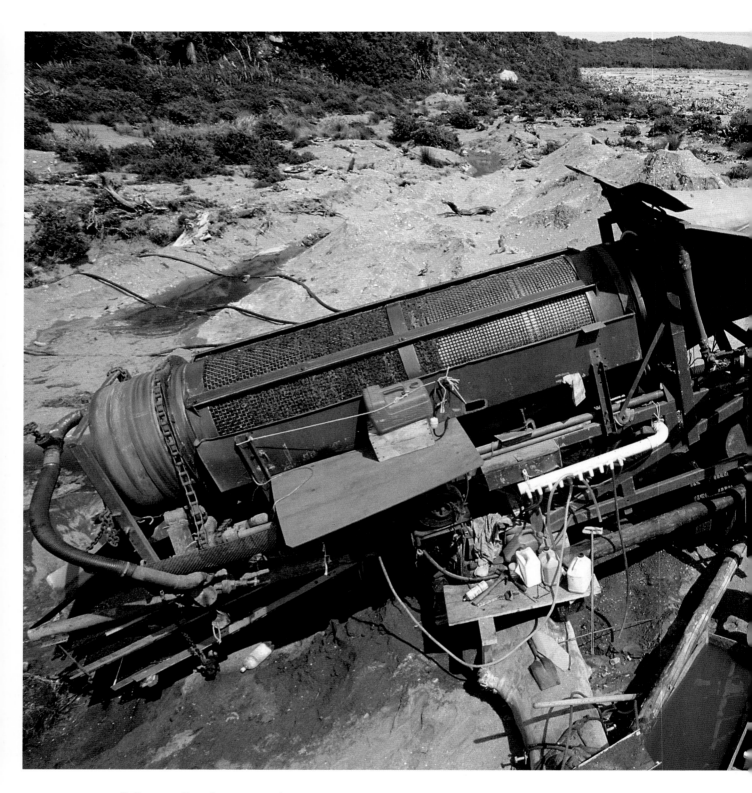

Gillespies Beach is part of a rocky coast
that was once part of the gold rushes,
and the allure of the precious metal still
calls back resolute goldpanners.

The West Coast combines superb
natural beauty with an immense
diversity of flora — some of the species
in Westland National Park date back
over 160 million years.

The perfect reflections of Westland's
Lake Matheson in early morning light.

The West Coast is renowned for its extraordinary weather and skyscapes. Cloud swirls over Mt Tasman (below), and a rainbow emerges after a shower (right).

Winter landscape near Lindis Pass.

Dunedin and Otago

Otago is a place of mountains, lakes and glaciers. Most striking are The Remarkables, near Queenstown, but equally lovely are the mountains around Lakes Hawea, Wanaka and Wakatipu, where glaciers ground the hills into rounded shapes before the time of man. Then there is the Clutha, a river of immense strength, storming through steep gorges to the sea.

Queenstown is New Zealand's best-known mountain resort. An area of unsurpassable beauty, it is also a centre for adventure activities — jetboating, rafting, tramping, heliskiing or, for those who don't mind being tied by the ankles, the ultimate thrill — bungy jumping.

The earliest Europeans in Otago were whalers. As with Christchurch, however, settlers soon realised the potential of the alluvial plains, and in 1848 the ships *John Wickliffe* and *Philip Laing*, with three hundred settlers aboard, arrived in Otago Harbour. Primarily Presbyterian, the Scottish founders established Dunedin on the fortunes of great sheep stations. The discovery of gold boosted the city's coffers and, by 1871, one in every four settlers in New Zealand was to be found in Otago. By the 1880s Dunedin was the country's largest, most industrialised and pre-eminent commercial city. Although this is not the situation today, Dunedin still exerts considerable influence nationally.

Dunedin has the reputation of being the Edinburgh of the South, the result of its Scottish heritage. Constructed of grey stone, it is a handsome city, with many buildings that are perfect Victorian artefacts. Everywhere there are church spires topping churches of austere Gothic grandeur. The Municipal Chambers display a frontage in the Italian style, while the architecture of the law courts, the railway station and the university attest to a Victorian exuberance muted by a sense of respectability.

Throughout Otago there are still signs of a prosperity based on whaling, sheep rearing and gold. Otago's greatest treasure, though, is its unique landscape.

Lake Wanaka (above and centre left) and Lake Hawea (bottom left) are water-filled glaciated valleys, the result of glacier action that has smoothed and rounded the landscape below the surrounding peaks.

Rosehips and willows grace the
Matukituki river valley.

Originally a gold-mining settlement, Cromwell originally sat on the confluence of the Clutha and Kawarau rivers. In 1992 its commercial centre vanished beneath the waters of Lake Dunstan when it formed behind the Clutha Dam. The town now rests within a lakeside surround. The region around Cromwell is renowned for its fruit-growing ability, particularly apricots and nectarines.

Mustering time at Loch Linnhe Station,
near Queenstown. Meanwhile, on the
banks of Lake Wakatipu, sheep briefly
take precedence on the road.

Queenstown is the home of adventure,
with bungy jumping and jet boating two
of its major attractions.

If a jump from the historic Kawarau
Bridge doesn't appeal, you can take a
gondola ride up to Bobs Peak, high
above Queenstown.

TSS *Earnslaw* is the last of four steamers that plied Lake Wakatipu during the height of the gold rush days. Queenstown nestles on the edge of the lake.

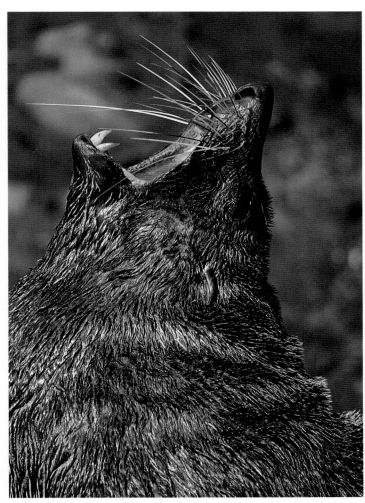

A sea lion, glistening sovereign of the seashore, roars at Moeraki Peninsula. The Moeraki coastline is steeped in Maori history, and the famed Moeraki boulders, each weighing several tonnes, are said to be the petrified food baskets of an early canoe which was wrecked on the offshore reef.

Taiaroa Head is the home of a famous
Royal Albatross colony. Also on the
Otago Peninsula is the imposing Otakou
Marae. A scenic rail journey in this part
of New Zealand must take in the craggy
Taieri Gorge.

The University of Otago was the first university in New Zealand. The old part of the building was begun in 1870.

Larnach's Castle, built in 1871 by a wealthy banker who later became a Member of Parliament, is notable for its impressive ballroom, ornate ceilings and Italian marble fireplaces.

Dunedin Railway Station, built in 1907, is embellished with an impressive tower, magnificent mosaic floor, and stained glass windows with a distinctly 'railways' theme.

Olveston is an Edwardian residence that conjures up the elegance of a bygone era, beautifully furnished with antiques, fine paintings and memorabilia.

Lush ferns in a remote Fiordland
setting.

Murihiku: The South

The southern end of Aotearoa is known to the Maori as Murihiku, and encompasses Southland, Fiordland and Stewart Island. Southland's history is similar to that of Otago. Invercargill was settled by Scots people from Dunedin in 1856, and the Scots heritage is still noticeable in the way Southlanders speak; there is a distinct burr on their r's. The new settlers found Southland similar to the Scottish highlands, and they established sheep runs on the Southland plains.

Bluff is the harbour from which agricultural produce is sent to all parts of the globe. It is also a vigorous fishing port, with catches of deep-sea fish, crayfish and shellfish. The Bluff oyster is considered by connoisseurs to be the ultimate in oysters.

Offshore from Invercargill is Stewart Island, a special place of bush-clad hills and quiet beaches. The Maori name is Rakiura, a reference to the glowing skies and auroras which play on the southern horizon.

West of Invercargill the vista opens out to the unparalleled beauty of Fiordland National Park. Sea and the massive forces of the Ice Ages have created astounding physical configurations to the land. Every day rain, wind, cloud and sleet combine to recreate an everchanging panorama. Along the coast are the great fiords — Milford, Bligh, Caswell, Nancy, Doubtful, Dusky and Preservation Inlet. Inland are the Takitimu Mountains and the lakes Te Anau and Manapouri, and the magnificent Milford Track, a walk which has been called the finest in the world.

The superb Catlins coast has a rugged
grandeur that, once experienced, is
never forgotten.

Nugget Point lighthouse surveys a rocky coast. In contrast, the small church at Waikawa is serene in the sunshine.

Sheep shearing is a fast and furious
business — definitely not for the faint-
hearted.

A field of wild flowers on the road to
Milford Sound. Milford is dominated by
Mitre Peak, rising steeply from the deep
waters of the fiord.

Trampers experience all types of conditions on the 54-kilometre Milford Track, often described as 'the finest walk in the world'. The magnificent Bowen Falls drop down into Milford Sound.

Dawn at Cascade Cove, Dusky Sound,
and half-light at Acheron Passage.

Doubtful Sound, named Doubtfull
Harbour by Captain Cook in 1770, is
one of the most haunting of the
numerous southern fiords. Nearby,
morning mist hovers over the rainforest.

A playful dolphin leaps before the
Milford Wanderer, scouting across the
mist-shrouded waters of Dusky Sound.

No matter where you are, you will
always find surfers chasing the waves,
even here at Oreti Beach, among the
most southern waves of the world.

The tuatara, often called New Zealand's living dinosaur. Southland Museum in Invercargill has the country's most successful breeding programme.

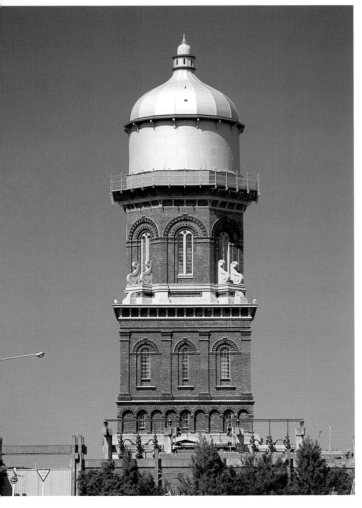

During the late 1800s Invercargill was known as the 'City of Fires' as a result of low water pressure that hindered firefighters. The Invercargill water tower, opened in 1889, was utilised for its intended purpose until the 1930s when it was relegated to a back-up role until the 1990s. It is now a protected building and is a reminder of the city's early engineering feats.

The port of Bluff welcomes visitors into this southern seafaring town. The area has an expanding export trade and is the base for boats that dredge the Foveaux Strait for world-famous Bluff oysters. The oyster season is celebrated with an annual week-long festival that includes oyster-opening and oyster-eating competitions.

Fred and Myrtle Flutey's house, in Bluff,
celebrates the beauty of the paua shell
in a unique and fascinating way.

Stewart Island is a special place. Remote and sparsely populated, it has great appeal to trampers and others seeking peace and tranquillity. It also supports a vigorous fishing industry.

Stewart Island's Maori name is Rakiura,
aptly translated as 'island of glowing
skies'.

Acknowledgements

Thank you to the many New Zealanders who welcomed me to Aotearoa and made me feel at home.

And thank you, friends and fellow travellers, for the inspiration and the best of times. You know who you are.

— H.L.

Thanks to Montana Wines Ltd and Air New Zealand for travel assistance in the South Island, and to Holger Leue, Ian Watt, Susan Brierley, Chris Lipscombe and Alison Jacobs.

— W.I.